I0100760

#BLACKLOVE:

CONVERSATIONS THAT STRENGTHEN RELATIONSHIPS

STEPHAN AND ALEXIS BLOUNT

#BlackLove: Conversations that strengthen relationships

© 2022 By Stephan And Alexis Blount

All rights reserved. No portion of this publication may be reproduced, stored in a retrieval system, or transmitted in any form or by any means–electronic, mechanical, photocopying, recording, scanning, or other–except for brief quotations in critical reviews or articles, without the prior written permission of the publisher.

Published in Hampton, VA, by Fruition Publishing Concierge Services. Fruition Publishing Concierge Services is a division of Alesha Brown, LLC.

Fruition Publishing Concierge Services can bring authors to your live event. For more information or to book an event, visit Fruition Publishing Concierge Services at:

www.FruitionPublishing.com

ISBN: 978-1-954486-03-4 Paperback

ISBN: 978-1-954486-04-1 eBook

Library Of Congress Control Number: 2021901682

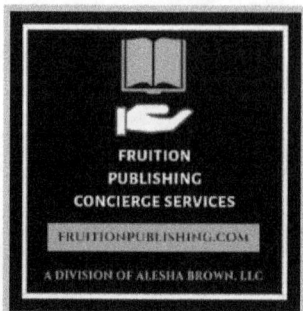

FRUITION
PUBLISHING
CONCIERGE SERVICES

FRUITIONPUBLISHING.COM

A DIVISION OF ALESHA BROWN, LLC

TABLE OF CONTENTS

1. The Truth About Black Love   1

2. Submission   7

3. Singleness   17

4. Keeping The Flame Alive & The   23
   Importance Of Dating Your Spouse

5. Childhood Traumas   25

6. Prayer and Inviting God On Your   29
   Relationship Journey

7. Success - Ride Or Die   33

8. So What Makes Black Love So   37
   Challenging?

9. What Makes Black Love So Special   43
   And Unique?

10. How Does God Fit In The Strength   49
    And Longevity Of Black Love?

11. Do Not Settle   55

12. Keeping One Another First And Still   59
    Achieving Goals And Dreams While
    Being Young Parents

13. Your Resolution   63

    References   69

CHAPTER I
THE TRUTH ABOUT BLACK LOVE

B lack love is unique and like no other. And while our couples and singles will share with you the amazing beauty of black love and the lessons they have learned, statistics show the battle for love in the black community.

According to the U.S. Census[1], in 2009, 71 percent of black women in America were unmarried. Of that group, 71 percent of black women between the ages of 25 and 29 and 54 percent between 30 and 34 had never been married. By comparison, 43 percent of non-Hispanic white women between the ages of 25 and 29 had never married.

While these statistics are startling to some, others will use them to validate why they are single and struggling to find their spouse. Before we proceed, let's discuss the truth of these statistics and dispel four common myths about black love, courtesy of ThoughtCo[2].

- **Black Women Don't Marry.** A Yale University study found that just 42 percent of black women are married, and a variety of high-profile news networks such as CNN and ABC picked up that figure and ran with it. But researchers Ivory A. Toldson of Howard University and Bryant Marks of Morehouse College question the accuracy of this finding:

"The often-cited figure of 42% of black women never marrying includes all black women 18 and older," Toldson told the root.com. "Raising this age in an analysis eliminates age groups we don't really expect to be married and gives a more accurate estimate of true marriage rates."

Toldson and Marks found that 75 percent of black women marry before they turn age 35 after examining census data from 2005 to 2009. Plus, black women in small towns have higher marriage rates than white women in urban centers such as New York and Los Angeles, Toldson remarked in the *New York Times*.

- **Educated Black Women Have It Harder.**
News stories about black marriage often mention that more black women pursue higher education than black men—by a 2-to-1 ratio, according to some estimates. But what these articles leave out is that white women also earn college degrees more than white men do, and this gender imbalance has not hurt white women's chances at matrimony. What's more, black women who finish college actually improve their chances of marrying rather than lower them:

"Among black women, 70% of college graduates are married by 40, whereas only about 60 percent of black high school graduates are married by that age," Tara Parker-Pope of the *New York Times* reported.

The same trend is at play for black men. In 2008, 76 percent of black men with a college degree married by age 40. In contrast, only 63 percent of black men with just a high school diploma tied the knot. So, education increases the likelihood of marriage for both African American men and women. Also, Toldson points out that black women with college degrees are more likely to marry than white female high school dropouts.

- **Rich Black Men Marry Outside Their Race.** By analyzing census data, Toldson and Marks found that 83 percent of married black men who earned at least $100,000 annually married black women. The same is true for educated black men of all incomes. Eighty-five percent of black male college graduates married black women. Generally, 88 percent of married black men (no matter their income or educational background) have black wives. This means that interracial marriage should not alone be held responsible for the singleness of black women.

- **Black Men Don't Earn As Much As Black Women.** Black men are more likely than black women to bring home at least $75,000 annually. Also, double the number of black men than women make at least $250,000 annually. Because of pervasive gender gaps in income, black men remain the breadwinners in the African American community.

These numbers indicate that there are plenty of financially secure black men for black women. Of course, not every black woman is looking for a breadwinner. Not every black woman is even seeking marriage. Some black women are happily single. Others are gay, lesbian, or bisexual and were unable to legally wed those they loved until 2015, when the supreme court overturned the ban on gay marriage. However, the forecast for heterosexual black women searching for marriage, is not nearly as gloomy as reported.

For the singles reading this book, may you find hope in the valuable lessons shared within. For the engaged and married couples, regardless of the current state of your relationship, may you find inspiration from the couples within to strengthen your relationship.

Please remember to leave a review on Amazon.

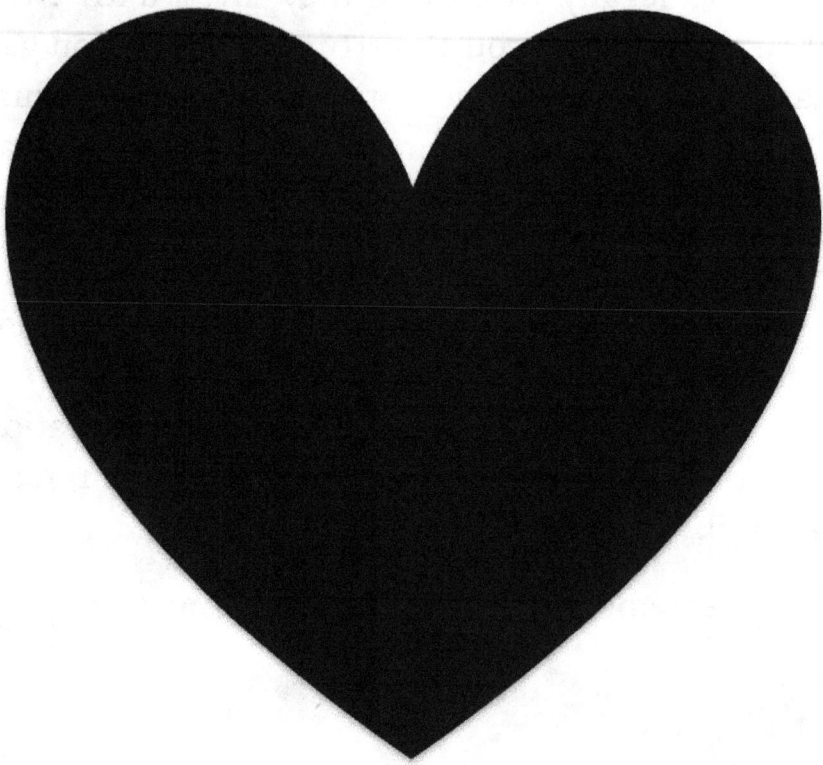

CHAPTER 2
SUBMISSION

L et's talk about the "s" word: **submission**. Although not everyone reading this book is married or aspires to marry, submission is a part of long-term relationships and starts before marriage. #truthbomb

Before we continue, share your thoughts on submission below and then continue onto the next page so we can continue this discussion:

Q: What comes to mind when you hear the word "submission?"

_____

_____

_____

_____

_____

Q: Have you seen healthy examples of submission in relationships you know?

_____

_____

_____

_____

_____

Q: What lessons were you taught as a child about submission?

_____

_____

_____

_____

_____

Q: As an adult, what role does submission play in your relationships?

_____

_____

_____

_____

_____

In many marriages, submission may naturally take place, and sometimes it happens organically. For some couples, it is something that has to be discussed.

Submission: *an act or instance of submitting, or yielding control to a more powerful or authoritative entity*[1].

Couples need to talk about what submission means to them to better understand what it will look like in their relationship. This is especially true if one or both of them were raised in a single-parent home. What some people fail to realize is that submission does not always mean the woman is submitting to the man. Sometimes, the man is submissive to the woman.

Biblically, the wife must submit to the husband, and the husband shall submit to God. And while that is very cut and dry when you do your biblical research, there are no guidelines anywhere about how to properly submit to a boyfriend/girlfriend or even a fiancée/fiancé.

There is a fine line between knowing that the guy will be your husband or knowing the woman will be your wife but not wanting to come off as trying to do too much before it is time. (Has this been a problem for you in the past?)

What time frame is appropriate to start biting your tongue or putting your foot down? How do you do that without holding everything in until you erupt? Simply keeping quiet and keeping your head down is not submission. It can all become overwhelming and, if we are transparent, it can lead to a lot of opposition and adversity within a perfectly good relationship.

While preparing for marriage, a couple has to play some sort of house (appropriately) to see how and if they can function together. I mean, how else will one know if the partner is their cup of tea?

The thing is, "submission" can be a term that turns people off or get them turned up because of how it is perceived in contemporary culture: the implication that women are inferior to men. This inferiority is the furthest thing from the truth.

Women are not inferior. We are to submit to one another as reverence for Christ. That is the goal. No one is a doormat; no one is less than.

Disclaimer: How you and your partner choose to operate is entirely up to the two of you and should be discussed early on in the relationship and, as you grow and change on your journey, the dynamic will change.

Maybe your views on submission will change. The key is to communicate and share where you are.

Husbands are to love and respect their wives; boyfriends should love and respect their girlfriends. Fiancés should love and respect their fiancées and vice versa.

Biblical submission allows a wife to **confidently** follow her husband's lead. This cannot be done if the relationship's foundation is not built on love and respect. The confidence that a woman needs to do this does not start after "yes" or "I do." This confidence is built while dating, which is why the dating phase is so imperative.

Rushing to the ring or chapel will only cause you to miss out on the important developmental stages necessary to build a happy and healthy marriage. You can compare this to taking a cake out of the oven before it is done. The flavor is there, but when you stick a toothpick in it, some parts are still runny. The cake needs to bake more. (Are you a victim of an "ill-baked" type relationship?)

Let Your Relationship Bake. Marriage is free will, and God honors marriage. God also honors relationships.

A husband being a leader of the home makes him the head and puts great responsibility on him. God expects specific behaviors from the husband as the head or leader of the house. However, husbands are not to mistreat their wives as it is clear that they are to treat and love their wives as Christ loves the church.

Husbands should even be willing to die for their wives if necessary. They are not to belittle their wives or rob them of their identity.

Men: can practice strengthening their relationship with God and honoring Him as their headship.

Women: can practice praying for their boyfriends when problems arise versus mouthing off and saying hurtful things because they think they are right and the boyfriends are wrong.

Now I can hear some of you thinking that I have lost my mind. Some of you feel that submission is old school, outdated, and not a reality today. But you are wrong. Not only is submission natural, but all of us do it every day.

Case in point:

- Do you drive a car? You practice submission every time you yield to the other cars around you. Sure, you can go through the red light or just blindly change lines and have it your way, but you don't.

- Ever held the door open for someone? You have submitted to them, even when you do simple things like moving to the side and letting others have the right-of-way.
- Men: have you ever spruced up your bachelor's pad before bringing a date to your home for the first time? Submission!

These examples are different because you are not in a romantic relationship with the people, but the implication is still the same. Submission is a natural part of life and an essential part of any relationship.

Oh, and just for argument's sake, submission and obedience are not the same. The difference is probably why some of you have a problem with "submission."

Obey: *to comply with or follow the commands, restrictions, wishes, or instructions of*[2].

Let's delve into this. If you understand the power in the following words I share, you will not only feel empowered in your relationships but life in general. No relationship built on love is void of choices. Submission is a choice, and obedience is required based on the hierarchy of the relationship. Regardless of the type of relationship or your role in it, everyone has a choice.

First, you have the choice to be in that relationship or not. You had the choice to enter it, so you have the choice of whether to remain in it or leave. No choice should be taken lightly.

But several other choices exist throughout the different layers of the relationship over time. As I shared, in God's order, the husband is the head of the home, where the hierarchy applies. This is why the original vows included the words "obey." The wife is not the only person who must obey the head in the relationship: the head must obey God, who he leans on to lead the house. This is why marriage is a three cord strand that shall not be broken.

Submission is often thought of as something negative. It is not. Godly headship is loving, kind, and gentle, considering Christ in all things. The man that exhibits this form of headship makes it easier to submit to him than one who does not.

This is why, as we move to the next topic of *singleness*, you must **choose** wisely. A relationship where one has no choice, no control, is centered on manipulation, not love. This type of control is often confused with obedience and submission. Nothing could be further from the truth.

Any relationship where there is no way out is not centered on love, and God is love. We need God for any relationship we have. He must guide and lead us because he created us, knows us individually, and can advise the best way to deal with the other. God is also good at reminding us when we need to keep our mouths shut versus responding in the heat of passion or anger.

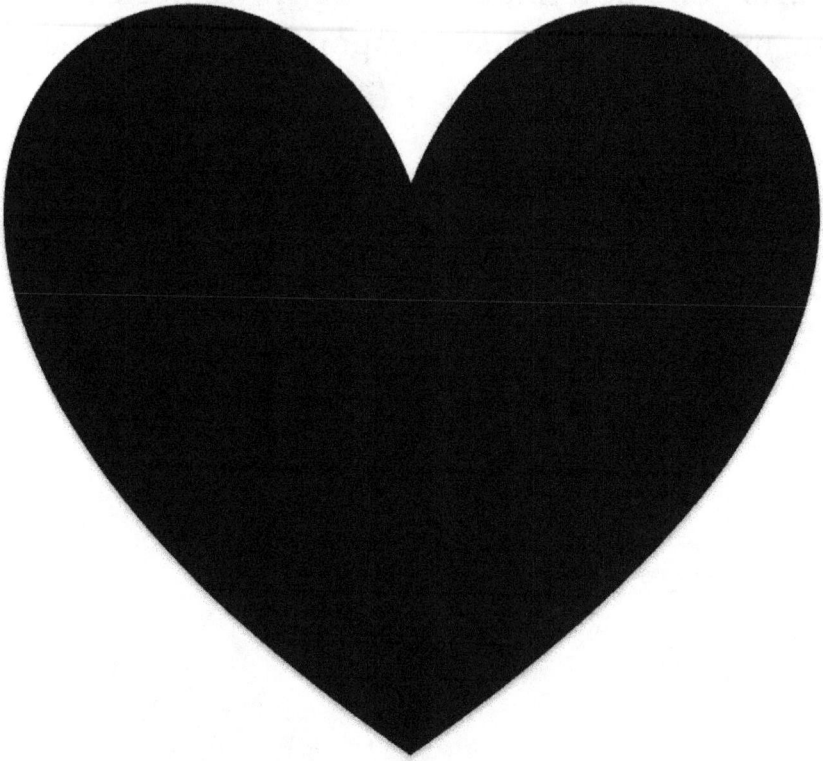

CHAPTER 3
SINGLENESS

Until legally married, you are considered single. Period. It's tight but right.

Regardless of whether you have been dating, living together, or even engaged, you are single. The length of time you have been together does not change your single status.

While living life as a single man or woman, it is important to put God and yourself first and constantly remind yourself never to settle. It does not matter if you have been in a serious relationship for five years or you are 40 and want children. Regardless of your situation or status, never lower your standards for **instant gratification**. This is known as settling.

Settling is a choice derived from **fear**, and if we choose to trust God, we should not make desperate or hasty moves. It is understood that there is a social stigma promoting commitment and where we should be by a certain age, but we must release ourselves from any expectation outside of what God has instructed us to do. Your worth is not tied up in your ability to marry or have children. You are enough by yourself! (Feel free to repeat that as many times as needed until you receive that in your spirit. You must know that you know!)

Before committing to marriage, it is okay to want to work on yourself. I challenge you to question your motives and challenge who you are. Forget about biological time clocks, fear of loneliness, and the perceived downfalls of being single. In time, you will see that those things you thought were disadvantages are working in your favor.

Q: What Do You Feel Are The Disadvantages Of Being Single?

_____

_____

_____

_____

_____

There are great benefits in waiting until it *feels right*. There is goodness in dating and in every phase of singleness, dating, engagement, and marriage. Each has its benefits.

Do not be in a rush to feel ready, and do not be bound to a relationship that does not feel like the right match.

Q: If you are single, what are some things you could improve about yourself?

_____

_____

_____

_____

_____

Q: What is your vision of the relationship you desire? What does it look like?

_____

_____

_____

_____

Q: Who do you need to be in this ideal relationship? How is that different in any way from the person you are now?

_____

_____

_____

_____

_____

Q: How do you define romance?

_____

_____

_____

_____

_____

Q: What is your definition of intimacy? What do you feel intimacy is not?

_____

_____

_____

_____

_____

Q: List things someone can do to make you feel appreciated or loved.

_____

_____

_____

_____

_____

Q: What can someone do to make you feel unappreciated or unloved?

_____

_____

_____

_____

_____

#BLACKLOVE:

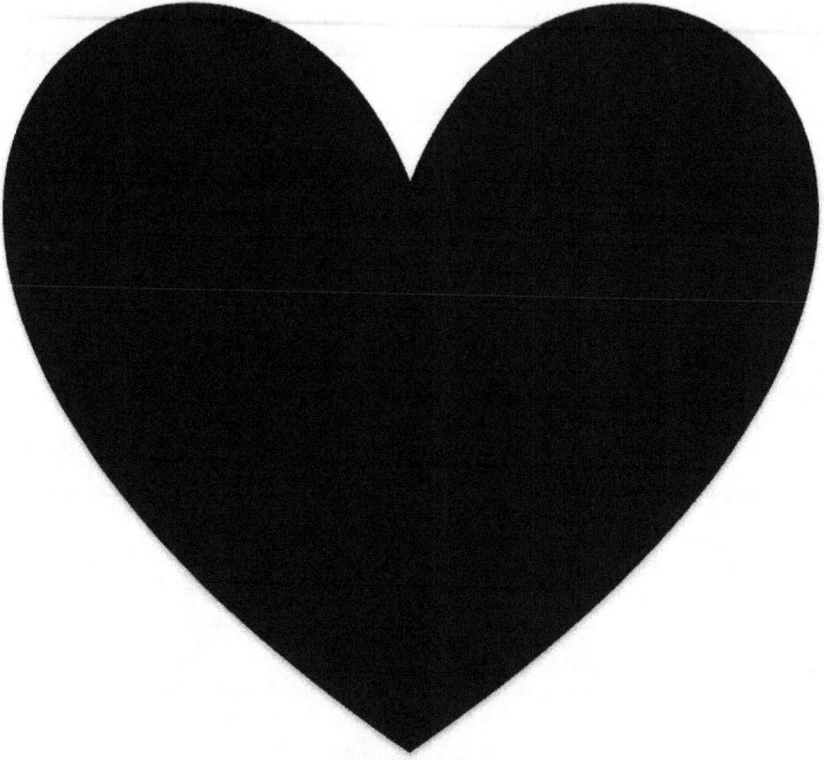

CHAPTER 4

KEEPING THE FLAME ALIVE & THE IMPORTANCE OF DATING YOUR SPOUSE

Remember your first crush? Remember the first time just seeing them pass by made your heart flutter, you became tongue-tied, or you wanted to faint anytime someone said their name? Well, I don't want to burst your bubble, but here is another #truthbomb:

At some point, for most, the butterflies go away.

Like a celebrity, if you could spend 24 hours a day, seven days a week with them, the infatuation would wear off. The fun, new, shiny toy would no longer be as exciting as it first was. I do not mean that you would no longer love them or occasionally feel that spark when you look into their eyes, but it might become less frequent than before.

The number of dates you have per month may decrease, and you often settle for a date every few months versus every week. When you add children, careers, and other responsibilities to the mix, it is easy to see how the flame starts flickering versus burning hot. The flame is dying and will soon go out if you let it get to that point. This is a huge no-no.

While dating, it is important to navigate the relationship according to how you want your relationship to be as a married couple (in some areas). **Begin with the end in mind.** It is imperative to stay romantic. Planning a night out on the town or a cute brunch date waters your relationship; those gestures will help your love grow. The memories you make together now will fertilize your marriage. Reflecting on the good times years from now will remind and encourage you to **date your spouse.**

No matter where life takes you, you will find joy reminiscing on the dating days. The memories will prompt you to keep dating and, believe it or not, date nights improve marriages and prevent divorce!

CHAPTER 5

CHILDHOOD TRAUMAS

The past will always haunt us if we do not address it properly. **You cannot confront what you choose to ignore.** Some of the things we experienced as children are tucked away in the back of our heads, and we feel like we don't have to deal with them. We will and, consequently, so will our partner. The person we choose to love and spend the rest of our life with will have to face our traumas head-on if we carry them (trauma) into our relationship or marriage, unresolved.

This is super heavy, right? Well, imagine carrying the baggage for another decade and trying to unpack it after years and years of toting it around. Or, even worse, what if the grudge takes over your heart and prevents you from loving those who love you?

The truth is this happens every day in the lives of those who have overcome trauma and abuse, especially during their formative years. Abuse and trauma's impact on interpersonal relationships is devastating for many survivors and can compromise their ability to form and maintain healthy relationships. Over time, this can take a toll on you and your partner. Some survivors have severe trust issues and avoid emotions or affections, while others may be overly attached or dependent.

This is not to say that you should avoid entering a relationship with a trauma or abuse survivor or feel as if you can never expect to have a healthy, loving relationship if you are a survivor. However, you must be aware we are a sum of our environment. In choosing to be with a person, you must take the time to learn about them and how each fits in the future you envision.

Q: What past events or traumas have you experienced that might affect your future relationship?

_____

_____

_____

_____

_____

Q: What type of things happened in your past relationships that you would never want to experience again?

_____

_____

_____

_____

_____

Q: Describe the type of relationships you saw in your childhood. Were they healthy or unhealthy?

_____

_____

_____

_____

_____

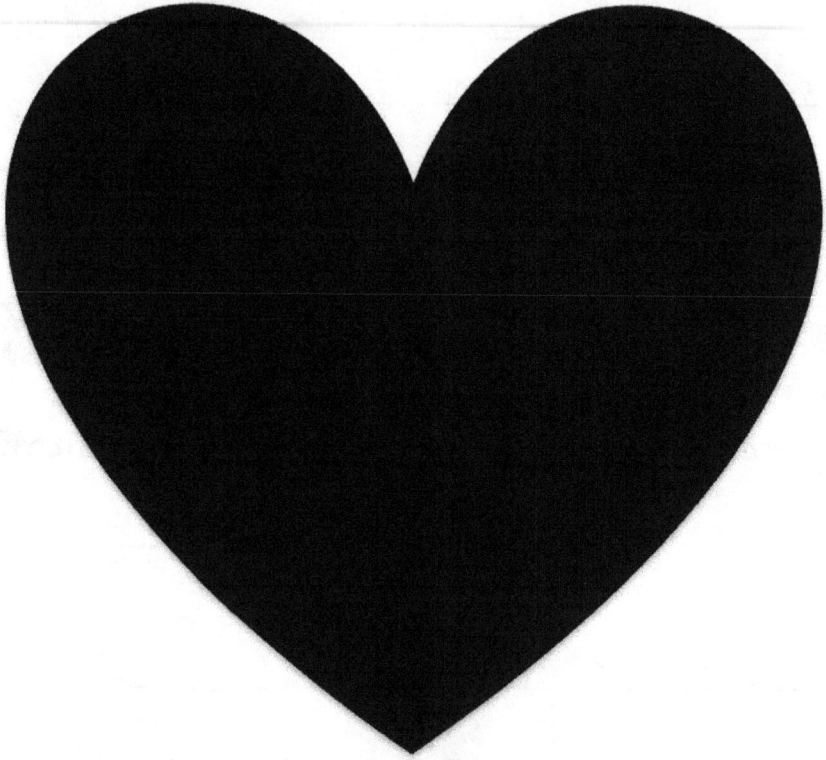

CHAPTER 6

PRAYER AND INVITING GOD ON YOUR RELATIONSHIP JOURNEY

We all like to believe that we are keeping God first in our lives, which is amazing. If we are being honest and completely transparent, most of us would agree that once we fall in love or start dating, our schedules shift, we spend our time differently, and, sometimes, our personal growth in Christ suffers. Such is life, and hopefully, we find a way to get back on track.

Sometimes the best way to continue giving God time while dating is to incorporate your prayer life into your current relationship. Adding bible study and church to the date night schedule can never hurt, right? Praying together will only strengthen your soon-to-be marriage.

Most people do not feel comfortable sharing their deepest prayers and their most intimate conversations with God with other people. That is understandable, and you do not have to. Challenge yourself to pray for others or your partner and see where that leads you.

Keeping God involved in your dating life will only set you up for success. Working to please Him by trying your best to submit to His word will only bless your life.

Dress it up and make it your style. Being a devoted Christian couple does not have to "look" a certain way. God is in your heart, so allow Him to work within and let it shine on the outside.

Q: How large of a role do you believe spirituality should play in your relationship?

_____

_____

_____

_____

Q: What is your prayer life like? How could it improve?

_____

_____

_____

_____

_____

Q: Are you comfortable in asking your partner to pray with you? Are you comfortable in asking your partner to worship God together?

_____

_____

_____

_____

_____

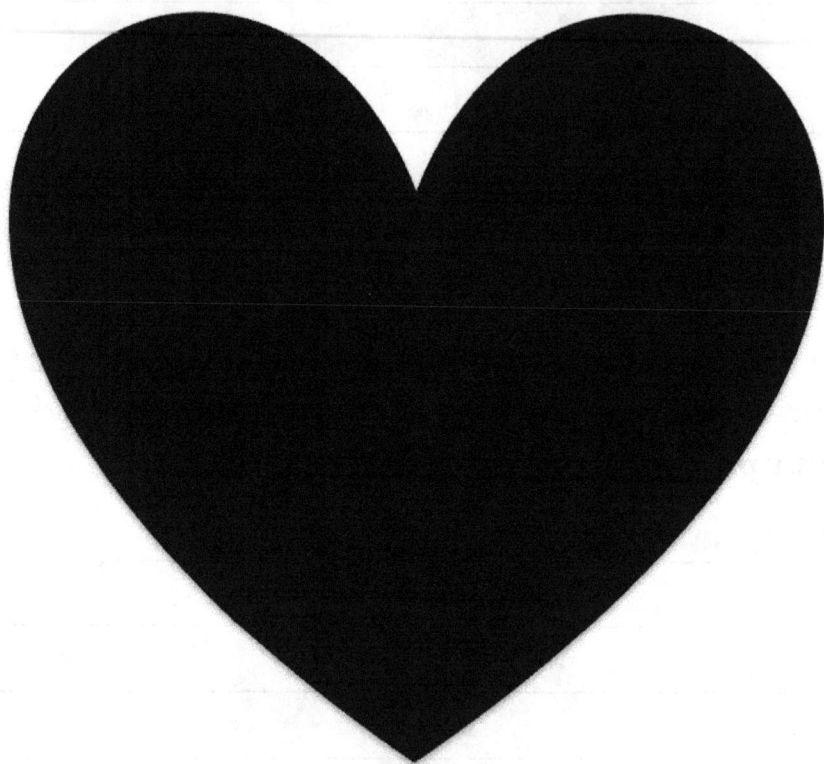

CHAPTER 7

SUCCESS - RIDE
OR DIE

There is nothing like a success story and having your partner beside you as your biggest cheerleader. We all know the **Bonnie and Clyde Story**, but here is the reality when it comes to relationships:

Real relationships go through a lot. Sometimes life hits you hard. Between careers, family, friends, and trying to grow personally, an individual's stress level can be overwhelming. However, knowing you have at least one true supporter can give you peace like no other.

Success in a relationship starts with transparency and honesty. No matter how bad the ugly truth seems, it should be shared. Before you can commit to being someone's *ride or die*, you must become that for yourself.

Let's be honest: many of us have done a poor job of being true to ourselves. We even speak poorly to ourselves at times and speak words of discouragement versus encouragement. While it is wonderful to have someone to support and lean on, sometimes you have to encourage yourself.

What do you want out of life? Even if kids, marriage, and family are the main goals you have (or may be a part of your life now), you are an individual. You have an identity separate and inclusive of these aspects. Sometimes, we become so consumed with catering to those around us that we put ourselves last. You cannot pour from an empty vessel or expect others to recognize when you need help and volunteer to help you. You must be your cheerleader and allow yourself to be of service to the ones you love.

Now back to this **ride or die**. Choose wisely, but give your lover the chance to decide if they are going to ride or die. Allow yourself the opportunity for someone to love you for your true self and all that comes with you.

Q: How do you define ride or die?

_____

_____

_____

_____

_____

Q: Are you willing to trust someone to be your ride or die?

_____

_____

_____

_____

_____

Q: If all else fails, can you be your ride or die?

_____

_____

_____

_____

_____

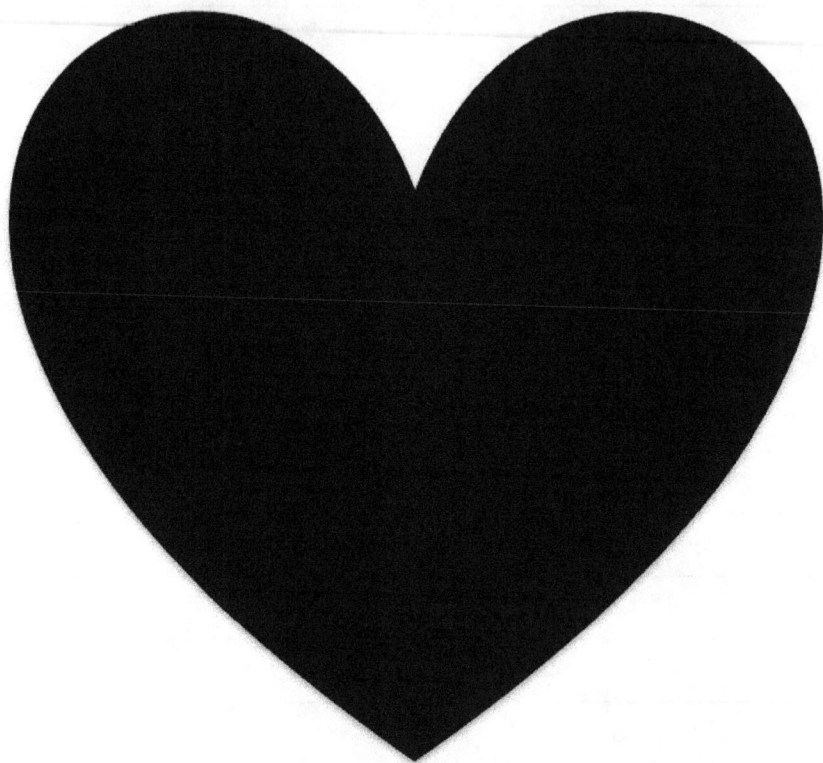

CHAPTER 8

SO WHAT MAKES BLACK LOVE SO CHALLENGING?

The world has painted this picture of black love as being nonexistent. The father is always missing, and the mother plays both roles when children are involved.

- Elisia Wright

There are a lot of factors that make black love challenging. From a historical perspective, the system is not built for our families and us to thrive and succeed. When couples do work, many times, the female is the breadwinner, which can make for a tense home environment if the black man is too prideful. When pride is removed, it can complicate some situations, but, in most cases, it is what pushes black love to greatness.

-Michele Pinellas

The ideal black couple in today's culture is rich and famous. Most individuals believe black love is Beyonce and Jay-Z or Ciara and Russel Wilson. Having this idea can limit someone from finding true love.

Someone's environment can make finding black love challenging as well. Venturing out from your everyday life can introduce you to your soulmate.

-Autumn Dickey

I don't feel as though black love is challenging, complicated, or rare. I feel as though everyone wants black love. You have to stop looking for it and just let it find you because it will when the time is right.

-Jabari Dickey

To be honest, you don't see what a healthy relationship looks like. So many black families do not have that. I think that's one of the environmental challenges that a lot of black people go through.

An added point to that is, with black love, you're raising black children as well, and you have to teach them the stigmas that are out there and how they can be treated differently. So that's a whole new thing; a curveball. Having an added variable of parenting is hard enough, but now you have something extra with black children.

-Kevin Ramos

Black people have had to fight through a lot of things. Like there are a lot of challenges that people had to go through. I don't know if I could compare it to every other race, but just from stories that I've heard, I know that it takes a lot to have a marriage last.

I think about the people who didn't have an example of black love. They're still fighting to have that, and they're figuring it out on their own. Then you have to think about the people who had an example, but it wasn't a healthy example because, again, those traumas have been passed down for so long. So unhealthy habits have been passed down, and you have to unlearn all of them. Unhealthy habits make marriage much more difficult.

It's not easy, no matter which way it goes—whether you were raised in a family of marriages or whether you weren't—there are just so many challenges. We're always fighting, always having to grow, unlearn, and just stay dedicated to pursuing this love that we know is possible.

-Antoinette Ramos

Sometimes you meet so many couples that have been married for 50 or 60 years. Just to sit back and listen to what they conquered, what problems they went through, and they still overcame. They still pushed through and remembered why they were together, what their purpose was as a couple, and why they married.

I think that's a cultural thing that black people do. We overcome anything. To implement love in that love with black people is beautiful. It can't be copied by anyone else.

-Quierah Caldwell

I think the beauty of black love is in our survival. When you look at us culturally, we have survived so much. I think that the beauty of that survival is interwoven within black love because you have two parties that understand that we are better together. And that's what black love is: we're better together. We're here to support one another and make sure that we are okay as a family.

- Stephen Caldwell

Q: Do you think Black Love is challenging? How so?

_____

_____

_____

_____

_____

Q: Which comments above do you agree with? Why? Which ones do you disagree with? Why?

_____

_____

_____

_____

_____

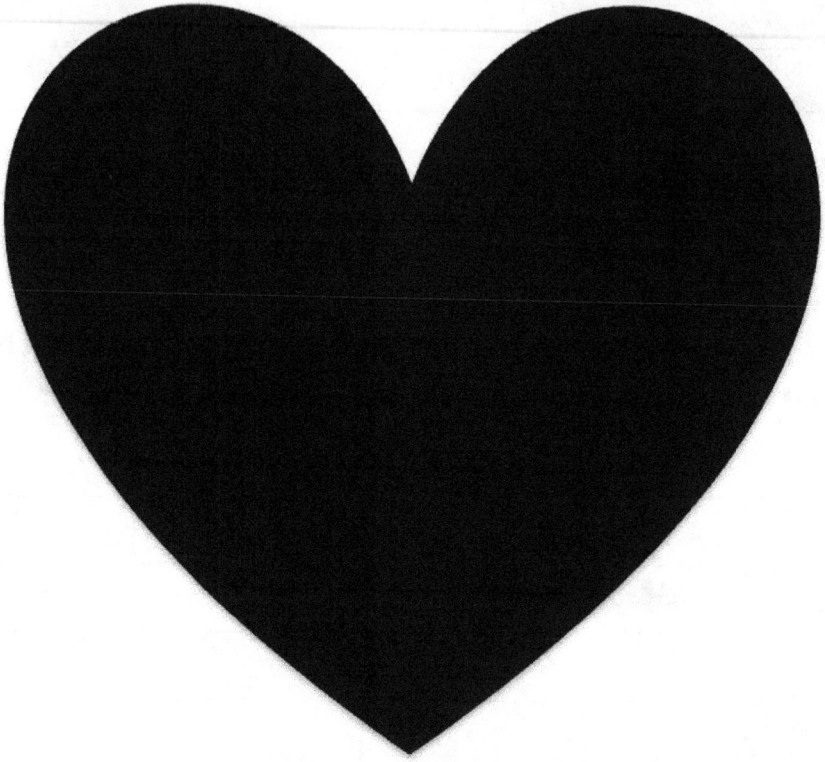

CHAPTER 9
WHAT MAKES BLACK LOVE SO SPECIAL AND UNIQUE?

With my Hispanic heritage, when I read this question, I think about the ability to love a black person in a world that pretty much belittles black people and makes them seem to be at the bottom of the totem pole or that they're less than the other races. I think it's so beautiful because you have to fight the mental seeds that have been planted in your head to say that black people are:

- Less Than
- Violent
- Not Good Parents
- Ghetto

There are so many stereotypes that the world tells us, especially in America. So for me to love my black wife is just beautiful because I know it's something true and internal that I had to fight through all those stereotypes and challenges.

-Kevin Ramos

I feel like black love is very special because it's hard to persevere through so much. If you look at the last 400 years of black people, you will see how we've had to go through so many struggles. I come from a family of long marriages, and I've seen the obstacles people had to face, and a lot of dysfunction.

There's just a lot of things through our bloodline that we had to endure and trauma passed down through generations and go through all of that and still have marriages surviving and lasting, and people still want marriage. It's just really beautiful to me because it hasn't been an easy road for black people, so I just love to be able to persevere and still find them willing to seek love. I love that.

-Antoinette Ramos

I think that what makes black love so special and unique is its history. For example, I know that I have some family members who married at 14 or 16, and they're still married. I think black people overall have overcome and conquered so much, and black love is the same thing.

-Quierah Caldwell

Black love is special because of the way that couples love and support one another. As a marginalized group, we are not often given images of successful black couples. When we do see it, it is almost like a unicorn sighting. You have encouragement from other black couples almost instantly because of black love.

-Michele Pinellas

Black love is everything to me. I was raised by a single mother, so I came from a broken family. I want to provide my children with something I never had: a two-parent household. My mom made sure I had what I needed and more, but nothing could fill the void of my absent father.

-Autumn Dickey

Black love alone is special and unique. In my eyes, black love is strength, resilience, covering one another, and never giving up on each other.

-Jabari Dickey

Q: Do you think Black Love is unique? How so?

_____

_____

_____

_____

_____

Q: How do your culture and upbringing play a part in your answer above?

_____

_____

_____

_____

_____

Q: Which comments in this chapter do you agree with? Why?

_____
_____
_____
_____
_____

Q: Which ones do you disagree with? Why?

_____
_____
_____
_____
_____

#BLACKLOVE:

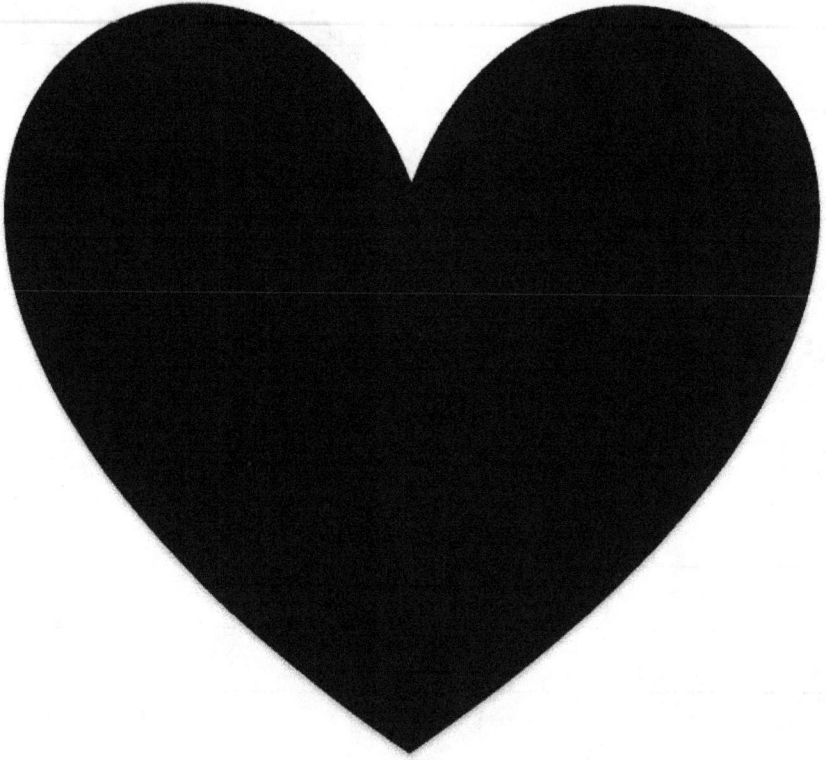

CHAPTER 10

HOW DOES GOD FIT IN THE STRENGTH AND LONGEVITY OF BLACK LOVE?

As humans, we are always evolving; we are always changing. God knows how He created your spouse. That spouse is also changing. God knows that changing person better than you do before you even knew them.

To keep it going, you have to keep going to God. To learn something about the spouse, the person that He created for you, takes time and persistence.

-Kevin Ramos

We believe that marriage was something that was created by God. God made Adam, and then He saw that it wasn't good for him to be alone, so He made Eve.

I think it's just really beautiful when you think that when the Father created you, He created another human being compatible with you, your missing piece/puzzle. That's why it's so important to know your maker and allow yourself to have that connection and relationship with God. Not only will you begin to understand yourself, but then you can ask Him to help you understand your partner.

That is how you can find the cheat code to having a long-lasting marriage, something that we're learning. We're just scratching the surface.

There is no better solution for sustaining a marriage than going to the person who created you both for each other. What else could be better?

-Antoinette Ramos

God should be the center of the relationship. Without God, the relationship doesn't have a solid foundation.

-Elisia Wright

God should be the cord that holds a marriage together. Many of the black couples that have lasted for years have mentioned this as well. God is the grounding principle and truly can be the secret to longevity. When things get rough, you pray. If things are going well, you pray. If you want things to get better, you pray. God is love.

-Michele Pinellas

God is in the center of our marriage. When we lived in Rhode Island for a year after we got married, we faced our hardest time as a married couple. Being across the country from our family challenged us but putting our faith and trust in God eventually got us back to Florida, where we currently reside.

-Autumn Dickey

God is the number one strength and longevity in our black love. God brought me my beautiful wife, and He has gotten us both through a very difficult time together and individually. I can't thank Him enough for bringing me a lovely angel, my wife.

-Jabari Dickey

Stephan is a pastor, and I am the first lady and worship leader. God is literally at the center of our love because, if God is not at the center, the puzzle would be incomplete. There would be a piece missing from the puzzle. In all things that we do, even if we're trying to decide on something, we talk about it with each other but also pray about it.

Literally, without God, we would not be anything. We would not be as strong as we are; there have been times that Stephan and I have almost broken up. There's been a time when the wedding was almost called off, but God reminded us of our purpose. He reminded us of why we are here and why He chose us for each other.

God is definitely there. He fits no matter how small or how little we are and what shape our puzzle may be. God fits regardless, and we move around that. He's at the center, an unmoving piece. With God in the center, we just fall in place.

-Quierah Caldwell

Make sure that God has shown you and led you to that person, and you're not just trying to be with that person for all of the physical attraction because that gets old. Let God guide you like God guides you.

- Stephen Caldwell

. . .

Q: Do you think it's important to have God as the center in your relationship? How so?

_____

_____

_____

_____

_____

Q: In your past (and present if you are currently in a relationship), has God been the center of your relationship?

_____

_____

_____

_____

_____

Q: If God has not been the center of your relationship and you believe He should be, what will it take for you to put Him there?

_____

_____

_____

_____

_____

Q: What will it take for your partner to be in agreement and for you both to work to make God the center of your relationship? (You cannot do this alone.)

_____

_____

_____

_____

_____

CHAPTER II
DO NOT SETTLE
BY ELISIA WRIGHT

Your person is out there and is praying for you. Until you meet your forever person, spend time becoming your best self. Work on being the person that you would want your spouse to be. Don't fall in love with potential, but see that person for who they are, face value.

If I would've compromised who I am and what I want in a man, I would've been dealing with things that God did not intend for me to deal with. Let me explain.

Boyfriend #1 was consistent, hardworking, independent, and loyal, but he didn't believe in God. His beliefs and thought process were completely different from mine, right down to the way we wanted to raise kids.

I probably wouldn't be as close to God as I am now if I had stayed in that relationship. My beliefs probably would've wavered. When you're constantly around someone, their ways can start to become your ways. That's why it's very important to watch the company that you keep. 2 Corinthians 6:14 (ESV) says: "Do not be unequally yoked with unbelievers. For what partnership has righteousness with lawlessness? Or what fellowship has light with darkness?"

Boyfriend #2 was goofy, funny, career-driven, family-oriented, and believed in God. He thought he wanted a God-fearing woman but soon realized that was not what he wanted. He was looking and comparing the relationship his mom and dad had and tried to apply it to ours; that simply did not work. He wanted to pick and choose what he wanted to honor from the Bible. Don't get me wrong, he wasn't a bad person or a bad boyfriend, but our differences started to create problems within our relationship. I had a stronger relationship with God than he did.

Compromising who I am to be in a relationship with him would've meant no longer paying tithes and offerings, going to church occasionally, and drinking alcohol. This is what being a lukewarm Christian looks like, which is dangerous. The Bible says in Revelation 3:15-16 (ESV): "I know your works: you are neither cold nor hot. Would that you were either cold or hot! So, because you are lukewarm and neither hot nor cold, I will spit you out of my mouth." I don't know about y'all, but I'd rather be kept by God.

Boyfriend #3 was caring, loyal, and honest. But he smoked all of the time, believed in God but still wanted to have premarital sex, wasn't open to celibacy, and wasn't trying to change his mind. He was unapologetic and wasn't changing for anyone. I was trying to change him into the man I wanted him to be. Mind you, I never wanted to be in a relationship with him. I was just having fun and enjoying our conversation.

Talking to him allowed me to put a band-aid on my problems and not fully heal from them. I saw potential in him and stayed in the relationship because of what could've been. Thank God I started seeing everything for what it truly was. If I had stayed in that relationship, I would've been unhappy. In so many words, I was telling God that I was fine with what I had, and I didn't want His best for me.

Boyfriend #4 believed in God but also had a relationship with Him. He had a strong prayer life and was intentional about his relationship with God. He was someone that I could've married and started a family with. However, it didn't play out that way. I think both of us have more growing to do, and although I believed I was born ready to be someone's wife, that was not true.

What keeps me from settling is knowing that God has created someone specifically for me. I don't ever want to look back and say: "What if?" I know that I won't have to compromise the person God has called me to be and that the person who is for me will add to me. We'll break generational curses together and live in purpose.

Q: In relationships, how have you settled?

_____

_____

_____

_____

_____

Q: If you are currently in a relationship, are you settling? How so?

_____

_____

_____

_____

_____

CHAPTER 12

KEEPING ONE ANOTHER FIRST AND STILL ACHIEVING GOALS AND DREAMS WHILE BEING YOUNG PARENTS

BY DR. MICHELE PINELLAS

My commitment to our family exceeds any of my personal goals. All I do and pursue professionally is to ensure that our family and our children can live the lives that my husband and I were not given as children. I have kept my family as my focal point throughout all of my accomplishments. At times, this has caused me a great deal of stress, but I know that they are rooting for me to win.

Having a blended family is not for the faint of heart. In my and my husband's case, there was a great deal of baby mama and baby daddy drama to overcome. Over the seven years that we have been together, we have grown as parents and co-parents. We both have experienced disrespect from our children's other parents, which initially caused strain on our relationship. We found that in order to overcome this drama, we had to keep each other first and realize that we were fighting on the same side and everyone else was against us. This helped get us on the same page, helping our co-parent relationships work better.

The older that we get, the more we realize that if it is not in the interest of our three children, the drama is unnecessary. I enjoy being a bonus mom and my husband enjoys being a bonus dad. We have been able to grow and share holidays in a cordial manner, which in turn allows our children to experience their entire family without having to choose one side over the other. At the end of the day, our family blended will always win.

I became a mother at the age of 20. I was beginning my senior year at Florida A&M University, and I knew that having a child was not going to stop me from achieving my goals. I met my husband in the summer of 2013, and my son was eight months old. I knew that I wanted to devote myself to my now-husband solely based on the fact that he also had a child at a young age and because of the way that he took to my son. He accepted me as a package deal and, because of that, I continuously choose him daily.

While I cannot speak for him, I make it my mission to make sure that my husband knows he is important in my life and my son's life. We also have a daughter together, and the relationship they share is one that every daughter dreams of. The same love that my husband gives to my son, I strive daily to give to my bonus son.

At the end of the day, because my husband and I have decided to choose each other and fight for our family as a unit, we have been able to accomplish great things. We recognize that we have our own individual goals to accomplish, however, when we work on our goals as a married couple, we can achieve way more. As we get older, the importance of our blended family strengthens us. Ultimately, this is what binds our marriage–knowing that we are fighting daily to achieve our goals as they will benefit our family for the long haul.

Q: Do you think it is important to keep each other first in a relationship? How so?

_____

_____

_____

_____

_____

Q: Which describes your typical situation: you keep the other person first, but they do not do the same for you or vice versa? Please explain.

_____

_____

_____

_____

_____

Q: In a selfish society, do you think couples can realistically be selfless and put each other first?

_____

_____

_____

_____

CHAPTER 13

YOUR RESOLUTION

The singles and couples have weighed in. We have all shared our experiences, lessons learned, and best guidance to attract and keep the type of love you desire. But you can only receive what you believe. Now that you have had the time to read, review, and meditate on what was shared, it is your time to plan for a different type of relationship experience.

If you are single, I want you to know that it is not too late for you. It does not matter how many failed relationships you have had — if you grew up not seeing healthy relationships or the **perceived** lack of "your ideal partner" out there — you can still attract the love and relationship you desire.

If you are married or in a relationship, the same is true. If you acknowledge that you settled and are not in your ideal relationship, do not consider this a failure. I offer you no advice by telling you to stay in or leave your relationship. Only you can make that decision. I do, however, encourage you not to lose hope that it is possible to improve your relationship. There are all types of transformation/ success stories from couples who were at their last rope and were able to turn it around. This may be you and your partner or spouse.

There is also the reality that some things, including relationships, have run their course and must come to an end. If this is you, and God has confirmed this, we send you love, hope, courage, strength, and faith. Let the Lord guide you and keep you through the process of dissolution. Never allow others to make you feel ashamed, less than, or a failure for doing what is best for you. Never lose hope that the love and relationship you desire still exist for you, even if it is not in your current relationship.

We are all a sum of our past experiences, and our experiences play a huge factor in the success of our relationships. Refuse to feel like you are disadvantaged or incapable of having a healthy relationship because of these factors. Once you acknowledge them, you are fueled with knowledge on things to look out for, address, and turn into strengths. Ignoring and not doing your work will produce the opposite of what you desire. Stay encouraged and do your work.

-Stephan and Alexis Blount

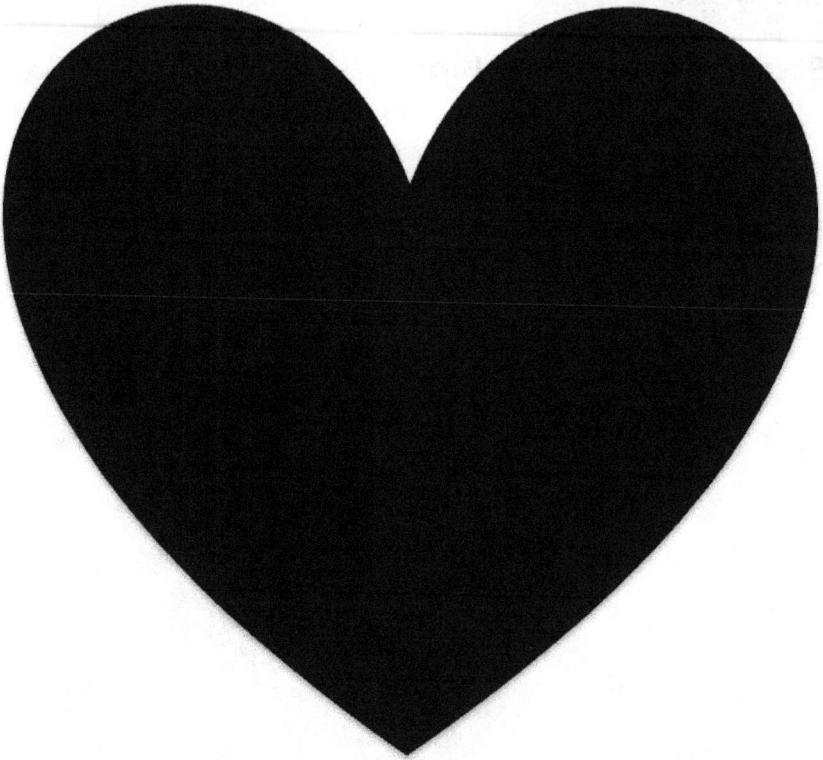

Q: Describe your ideal relationship.

_____

_____

_____

_____

_____

Q: Has your definition of an ideal relationship changed since reading this journal? If so, how?

_____

_____

_____

_____

_____

Q: What past experiences (including childhood) do you think put you at a disadvantage for having the type of relationship you desire?

Make a list below:

_____

_____

_____

_____

_____

REFERENCES

1. THE TRUTH ABOUT BLACK LOVE

1. Stewart, Dianne M. "Perspective | 2019 Marked 400 Years of 'Forbidden Black Love' in America." The Washington Post. WP Company, December 26, 2019. https://www.washingtonpost.com/outlook/2019/12/26/marked-years-forbidden-black-love-america/.
2. Nittle, Nadra Kareem. "The Top 4 Myths about Black Marriage." ThoughtCo. ThoughtCo, February 28, 2021. https://www.thoughtco.com/the-top-myths-about-black-marriage-2834526.

2. SUBMISSION

1. "Submission Definition & Meaning." Dictionary.com. Dictionary.com. Accessed June 23, 2021. https://www.dictionary.com/browse/submission.
2. https://www.dictionary.com/browse/obey.

www.ingramcontent.com/pod-product-compliance
Lightning Source LLC
Chambersburg PA
CBHW050230270326
41914CB00003BA/642